DIRK

BOGARDE

COMING OF AGE

PENGUIN BOOKS

PENGUIN BOOKS

Published by the Penguin Group. Penguin Books Ltd, 27 Wrights Lane, London W8 5TZ, England. Penguin Books USA Inc., 375 Hudson Street, New York, New York 10014, USA. Penguin Books Australia Ltd, Ringwood, Victoria, Australia. Penguin Books Canada Ltd, 10 Alcorn Avenue, Toronto, Ontario, Canada M4V 3B2. Penguin Books (NZ) Ltd, 182–190 Wairau Road, Auckland 10, New Zealand · Penguin Books Ltd, Registered Offices: Harmondsworth, Middlesex, England · This extract is from *Backcloth* by Dirk Bogarde, first published by Viking 1986. Published in Penguin Books 1987. This edition published 1996. · Typeset by Rowland Phototypesetting Ltd, Bury St Edmunds, Suffolk. Printed in England by Clays Ltd, St Ives plc · ·
10 9 8 7 6 5 4 3 2 1

From the early spring of 1944 until the end of the war in Europe in May 1945, Flt/Lt Christopher Greaves and I were joined at the hip as air photographic interpreters attached to 39 Wing of the Canadian Royal Air Force. I really don't remember where we were 'paired off', probably at Odiham airfield, but there we were, an unlikely couple in many ways, but as immutable as Laurel and Hardy, Huntley and Palmer, or Rolls and Royce.

Chris was senior to me by some years, had already had distinguished service in the RAF in Malta, survived the siege, contracted polio, and constantly fell in love with his nurses: he was, later, to marry one and raise a large family. But after Malta, and convalescence, he was stuck with me.

We had a truck which served as our 'office', with a couple of desks and lamps and not much else. In this, plus a jeep, we drove across Europe in the wake of our Forward Recce Squadron who took the photographs.

Being determined young men with great ambitions

the pilots had their airstrip as near the front as they possibly could be, dragging us, in consequence, along with them; for we had to be on hand for every sortie flown, ready to interpret.

I have often wondered, and did at the time, how Chris put up with me for so long. We were stuck together in that truck for hours and hours on end, and even when we did manage to get a break, usually when the weather was too bad for flying, we went off into the shattered countryside contentedly and painted. We never had a dispute or row, and remained together in work and in the snatched moments of leisure. We were a good team.

As I have said, the leisure was pretty nearly always in bad weather, which is why the great majority of my paintings had lowering skies, pouring rain and acres of mud and puddles. I never got to paint a sunny day – I rather doubt if I could have done so even if such a day had presented itself. I preferred 'mournful' light.

Chris was a professional artist; I only had the sparse training which I had gleaned at Chelsea Poly in between bouts of fumbling passion at the Classic cinema. But together we painted almost the entire campaign in Normandy, and were made Unofficial War Artists: our work belonged to the Air Ministry and was only returned to us after the German surrender.

At first, after the landings, there wasn't much time for painting anything. The early weeks were, to say the least of it, bewildering, on occasions unnerving. But as the Allied thrust got under way we started to settle in, knowing that we were there to stay until the end which, I was convinced, had to be in Berlin.

On the fortieth anniversary of D-Day, Chris telephoned from his home in the West Country.

'I don't know if you've been looking at telly today?' he said. 'Have you? Do you get that kind of thing in France?'

'All of it. I tuned in for ten minutes and stayed right through until the end.'

'Amazing, wasn't it? What about Mrs Reagan in that awful coat and NO hat! I mean, can you imagine a woman going to a memorial service without a HAT? Damned discourteous, I thought.'

'Oh well . . . it was all a long time ago, Chris.'

'Seemed just like last week to me, but then I'm getting ancient, I suppose. But you know, Pip, it was damned dangerous, wasn't it? If I'd have known how bloody awful it was going to be I'd never have gone!'

Fortunately for us both we neither of us thought

much of the danger at the time. Perhaps sheer youth takes care of that emotion, I don't know.

And Chris, who did most of the driving while I navigated, did some extremely dangerous things on our 'off days'. Driving along a wide stretch of open road along a ridge above the still-occupied town of Caen, shells fell behind and ahead of us, sending up ugly bursts of smoke and shrapnel.

'They're getting closer each time,' I said.

Chris was bent over the wheel of the jeep like a crouching charioteer, his cap had fallen off, his glasses glittered in the wet light.

'Bracketing us,' he said through clenched teeth.

One shell to the back, another to the front, each time the range was slightly altered. And they came nearer and nearer. It was extremely uncomfortable.

'Playing silly buggers.'

'So are we. Can't we get off this road?'

'You should know, you've got the map. I've got enough to do.'

There was no turn-off, the map shook and flapped, and was impossible to read. I only knew that when the shell behind us and the shell ahead of us landed simultaneously in the one place, we'd be dead centre.

 The spectacle, to the Germans below the ridge,

must have been amusing – although they are not a race noted for their humour.

But a single jeep belting along a dead straight road, silhouetted against the sky, as if the hounds of hell were after it, obviously proved an irresistible target for 'bracketing'.

A hawthorn hedge on the right of the road suddenly, providentially, was there and Chris swung into a field behind its sparse shelter of thorn and torn leaves.

We crawled out; lay flat in the crushed corn.

The Germans went on 'playing silly buggers' for about twenty minutes and then, mercifully, decided to give up. I couldn't help wondering, with each splintering crash, why they bothered to waste so much ammunition on so meagre and unimportant a target. Perhaps they thought we were Churchill? But in any case the German is always a very thorough creature.

Anyway, they stopped.

In the silence which followed the cease-fire, we crouched our way back to the jeep, inching across the trampled corn.

A group of Canadian soldiers suddenly rose as one man from a high-hedged bank, rifles cocked, mouths open in surprise.

'Where did you come from? For Chrissakes that's Jerry territory!'

'An error in map reading,' said Chris.

'I couldn't read the blasted map bucketing along like that with God knows what flying about. I honestly don't see the point in taking unnecessary risks, Chris, we've got quite enough to take without inventing more.'

'Rubbish.' Chris crammed on his cap and restarted the engine. 'A nice little country run. No need to get fidgety, old boy.'

So I shut up. It was all kids' stuff anyway. *Boys' Own Paper* nonsense.

Nothing to it. And we were still all in one piece.

Bigger and better things were ahead.

Two nights later we all stood in the shelter of the trees in the orchard, rocking and stumbling into each other, as wave after wave of giant bombers roared low over our heads and ripped the heart out of Caen.

We held on to each other, or the scaly trunks of trees. Showers of leaves and tiny apples shook around us as the earth rippled beneath our feet with the shock of the bombs which thundered down three kilometres away. The air trembled and rolled with the sound as

 if a thousand drums were beating a gigantic tattoo,

and the night was drenched in noise, drowning speech or even coherent thought.

We stood, heads bowed, eyes screwed up against the onslaught, grabbing about for support, like men drowning.

Ahead, through the trees, the whole skyline north of Caen was ablaze with white light, the clear night sky columned with enormous clouds of smoke and earth which barrelled upwards lit from the fires below, appearing to support a vast canopy of crimson cloud above the blazing town. A monstrous cathedral of flame.

With each shuddering blast, which seemed to suck the air upwards and leave us gasping for breath, the trees, in the light of the explosions, doubled themselves as leaping shadows, zigzagging against the dancing shapes of the tents. In the midst of the fury, a cow, maddened with terror, crashed among us trailing a broken rope at its neck, bellowing with fear, until it tripped in the guy-ropes and crashed to the ground under a sagging canopy of once-taut canvas.

There were no more Germans along the ridge road at Carpiquet to play at 'silly buggers' with a lone jeep: by the next day Caen had fallen and the battle for Normandy was almost over.

It was no time at all, I reckoned, for hermit crabs. All that, with so much else which I had devised for my personal protection, was cautiously set aside. Self-preservation and anonymity were, however, still uppermost in my mind. However, the former now took first place to the latter.

Strangely, I discovered in the first two months of battle that, though I was, indeed, often dry-mouthed with fear (or perhaps fright is a less craven word), at the same time the in-built eye of the observer was as alert as ever: I was curious, anxious to see, to experience, to be aware of the extraordinary things which were taking place about me.

And, in the letters to my father, to whom I wrote every week at least, if not twice a week, I was still 'keeping notes', just as I had done a thousand years ago in the Anthracite Years.

There was plenty of scope.

August that year, according to the letters which he had kept for me, appears to have been like a childhood summer: that is to say, eternal sunshine, cloudless, hot and clear.

The sky was always blue, that strange intense blue of northern France, sea-washed, wind-cleansed, limitless, criss-crossed with lazy scrawls of vapour trails like the idle scribbles of a child in a crayoning-book.

In the orchards the shade lay heavy beneath the trees, spiked here and there with emerald blades of grass and clumps of campion.

But everywhere the land was still. There was no birdsong.

Sometimes a bee would drone up and away, or a grasshopper scissor in the crushed weeds of the chalky soil, and then fall silent as if the effort had been too much, in the still heat, or as if, perhaps, reproved that there was no response in the ominous quiet.

No rabbits scuttled in the hedgerows, the corn stood high, ripe, heavy in the ear, unharvested, and in the meadows cows lay on their sides, stiff-legged, like milking stools, bellies bloated with gas.

Sometimes one of them would explode with a sound like a heavy sigh, dispersing memories of a lost childhood in the sickly stench of decay.

Death was monarch of that summer landscape: only the bee and the grasshopper gave a signal of life, or suggested that it existed. The familiar had become unfamiliar and frightening. A world had stopped and one waited uneasily to see if it would start again: a clock to be rewound in an empty room.

But that comforting tick-tock of normality, of the life pulse, had been provisionally arrested. In some cases it had been stopped for good, for a little further back, towards the beaches, they were burying those who would remain for ever in silence.

There was plenty of noise back there: of gears grinding, engines roaring, tracks rattling, metal groaning.

At the edge of an elm-fringed meadow, I stood against a tree watching, curiously unmoved, the extraordinary ballet between machines and corpses, which proved conclusively that the human body was nothing but a fragile, useless container without the life force.

For some reason it had never fully occurred to me before: I had seen a good number of dead men and had, as a normal reaction, felt a stab of pity, a creep of fear that perhaps it could be me next time, but I had become accustomed to them and got on with my own living.

But that afternoon in the shade of the elms I stood watching the bulldozers (a new toy to us then) shovelling up the piles of dead very much as spoiled fruit is swept into heaps after a market-day, and with as little care. Shuddering, wrenching, jerking, stinking of hot oil in the high sun, they swivelled slowly about with

 open jaws ripping at the earth to form deep pits, and

then, nudging and grabbing at the shreds and pieces, rotting, bloody, unidentifiable, which heavy trucks had let slither from raised tail-boards in tumbled heaps of arms and legs, they tossed them into the pits.

Back and forth they droned and crunched, swinging about with casual ease, manoeuvred by cheerful young men, masked against the stench and flies, arms burned black by the August sun.

'Tidying up,' said someone with me. 'One day they will turn this meadow into a war cemetery. Rows and rows of crosses and neat little walks; perhaps they'll erect a fine granite monument, a flagstaff will carry a proud flag to be lowered at the Last Post, they'll plant those bloody yew trees, and relatives will walk in silence through the toy-town precision and order, looking for their dead.'

I remember what he said, because I wrote it all down later, but I can't remember who he was.

Fairly typical of me, I fear.

The words stayed with me for the simple reason that they moved me more than the things which I was observing. The dead lying there in putrid heaps among the sorrel and buttercups didn't move me at all: they were no more than torn, tattered, bloody bundles. The soul had sped; there could only be regret for those who had loved the individual bodies in this seeping mass: for everyone there had once belonged to someone. That was the sadness.

The absolute anonymity of mass death had dulled grief.

The silence didn't last long – silence in war never does. One gets to discover that very early on.

The ominous stillness which had reproved both grasshopper and bee simply preceded a gigantic storm: Caen fell, the Germans began their terrible retreat to the east. The battle for Normandy was over.

I use the word 'terrible' advisedly, for the retreat, estimated at that time to be composed of at least 300,000 men plus vehicles and arms, crammed the dusty high-hedged roads and lanes, even the cart tracks through fields and orchards, in a desperate attempt to reach the ferries across the river Seine: the Allied armies surrounded them on three sides. We knew that all the main bridges had been blown, so it appeared evident to us that we contained the entire German fighting force in one enormous killing-ground. Tanks and trucks, horse-drawn limbers, staff cars, private cars, farm carts and all kinds of tracked vehicles, anything in fact which could move, inched along the jammed lanes and roads in slow convoys of death.

Unable to turn back, to turn left or right, they had no alternative but to go ahead to the river, providing undefended, easy targets for Allied aircraft which homed down on them as they crawled along and blasted them to destruction: ravening wolves with cornered prey.

By 21 August it was over.

Across the shattered farms, the smouldering cornfields, the smoking ruins in the twisting lanes, smoke drifted lazily in the heat and once again the frightening silence came down over a landscape of shattering carnage.

Those of us in the middle of things really thought that a colossal victory had been achieved. The Germans had been destroyed along with their weapons. There could be nothing left of them to fight, the Russians were about to invade their homeland, surely now victory was ours and the war would finish before the end of the summer?

We were wrong. The people who are in the middle are nearly always wrong. The canvas of war is far too great to comprehend as one single picture. We only knew a very limited part – and even that part was not as it seemed. Gradually we began to realize that the war was not over, that it was still going to go on, that the Germans were still fighting, still highly armed, stubborn and tougher than they had been before. Slowly 'a colossal victory' faded from our minds and we accepted the fact that something must have gone a little bit wrong in our jubilant assessment of an early peace.

It had indeed gone wrong. But it was only some years later, when the generals who had squabbled, quarrelled, and bickered all the way through the campaign began to write their autobiographies, that one learned that, far from a victory, the retreat had been a catastrophe.

By that time it was far too late for thousands of men to worry.

They were laid out in neat rows under white crosses.

What had happened, quite simply, is that the Allied generals, by disagreeing among themselves, had left the back door open to the killing-ground permitting thousands of Germans, and their arms, to escape and live to fight another day.

But we didn't know it, fortunately, at the time.

Standing in the aftermath of violent death is a numbing experience: the air about one feels torn, ripped and stretched. The cries of panic and pain, of rending metal, though long since dispersed into the atmosphere, still seem to echo in the stillness which drums in one's ears.

On the main road from Falaise to Trun, one of the main escape routes which we *did* manage to block, among the charred and twisted remains of exploded steel, dead horses indescribably chunked by flying shrapnel, eyes wide in terror, yellow teeth bared in frozen fear, still-smouldering tanks, the torn, bullet-ripped cars and the charred corpses huddled in the burned grass, it was perfectly clear that all that I had been taught in the past about Hell and damnation had been absolutely wrong.

Hell and damnation were not some hell-fire alive with dancing horned devils armed with toasting-forks. Nothing which Sister Veronica or Sister Marie Joseph had told me was true. Clearly they had got it all wrong in those early, happy Twickenham days. Hell and damnation were here, on this once peaceful country road, and I was right in the middle of it all.

My boots were loud on the gravel, oily smoke meandered slowly from smouldering tyres. Blackened bodies, caught when the petrol tanks of the trucks and cars had exploded, grinned up at me from crisped faces with startling white teeth, fists clenched in charcoaled agony.

Down the road in a haze of smoke stood a small boy of about seven; in his hand a tin can with a twisted wire handle.

I walked towards him and he turned quickly, then scrambled up the bank where a woman was bending over a body in the black grass, a hammer and chisel in her hand.

The boy tugged at her skirts, she stood upright, stared at me shading her eyes with the flat of her hand, then she shrugged, cuffed the boy gently, and bent again to her task.

Hammering gold teeth from the grinning dead.

The boy raised the tin for me to see. It was almost a third full of bloody nuggets and bits of bridge-work.

Waste not, want not.

In the ditch below us a staff car lay tilted on its side, the bodywork riddled with bullet holes in a precise line as if a riveter had been at work rather than a machine-gun from a low flying plane.

A woman was slumped in the back seat, a silver fox fur at her feet, her silk dress blood-soaked, a flowered turban drunkenly squint on her red head. A faceless man in the uniform of the SS lay across her thighs.

I kicked one of her shoes lying in the road, a wedge-heeled cork-soled scrap of coloured cloth.

The woman with the hammer shouted down, '*Sale Boche! Eh? Collaboratrice . . . c'est plein de femmes comme ça! Sale Boche!*'

I walked back to my jeep. My driver was sitting in his seat smoking.

'Where do they all come from?'

'Who?'

'Those blokes . . . wandering about having a good old loot. They just go through the pockets, get the wallets, pinch the bits of jewellery. There's a squad of women civilians in all this lot. Gives you a bit of a turn seeing dead women in this sort of set-up.'

Here and there, pulling at the blackened corpses, wrenching open the doors of the bullet-riddled cars, a few elderly peasants clambered about the wreckage collecting anything of value. God knew where they had come from – every building nearby was destroyed, but like the woman on the bank with the boy, they had come to scavenge what they could.

As we drove away the first bulldozers began to arrive to clear the road. I didn't speak: the sight of the dead girl with the red hair had distressed me profoundly.

I was prepared for people to be dead in uniform, but my simple mind would not come to terms with the sight of a dead woman in a silk dress on a battlefield.

That didn't seem to be right. They hadn't warned us about *that* on the assault course in Kent.

We had to pull aside to let a bulldozer grind past; I looked back and saw an old man dancing a little jig. In a fox fur cape.

Chris was kneeling on the grass before a five-gallon petrol can, sleeves rolled to his elbows, kneading a shapeless mass like a baker.

'What on earth are you doing?'

'Don't come near!' he yelled. 'If you light a cigarette we'll be blown to smithereens.'

'I'm not smoking. What are you doing?'

'Cleaning my uniform. Absolutely filthy.'

'So is mine.'

He dredged up a sodden battledress jacket. The smell of petrol was overwhelming.

'Just look at it! Black! Filthy!'

'Is there any particular reason why you want to clean the thing now?'

He looked up at me, dunked the jacket again, did a bit more kneading.

'Thought we might go to Paris,' he said. 'Can't arrive looking like a tramp.'

 'But it's not fallen yet . . . they're still fighting.'

‘Well, as soon as it stops. Couple of days’ time. Seems fitting.’

‘But it’s forbidden to the British. Only the Free French and the Yanks.’

‘Which is damned unfair, we’ve got every right to be there too, why not?’

On the morning of 26 August, almost before it was light, we set off in the jeep with the unexpired-portions-of-the-daily-ration, a painted paper Union Jack, which Chris had made and stuck on the windscreen, and a fairly taciturn driver who didn’t drink.

‘He’s essential,’ said Chris. ‘Teetotaller. We aren’t; and liberating Paris should mean a couple of glasses here and there. Got to get back in one piece.’

We liberated Paris: a celebration of the heart in an atmosphere of exploding gaiety and joy.

Driving back to the airstrip, just as evening nudged the edge of nightfall, I realized how wise Chris had been to bring a teetotal driver with us.

We’d never have got back without him.

Teetotal and taciturn he was; indeed he had hardly moved a limb, nor once smiled all day, among the tumultuous crowds of cheering and laughing people. His only comment, which almost brought us to complete sobriety, was: ‘These French haven’t got no control. Know what I mean? All over you before you can lift a finger to say bugger off – not so much as an "Excuse me". Bloody liberty! Foreigners! What can you expect?'

But he drove safely back through the dark while Chris and I assured each other solemnly that we had spent a really *most* agreeable day. A very agreeable day indeed. Probably the most agreeable day we'd had since the landings. *Certainly* so. A *splendid* day. We decided, after a mumbling silence, that we ought to liberate another city as soon as one became available.

We had our wish granted a week or so later when Brussels fell, and the unexpired-portion-of-the-daily-ration, wrapped in a sheet of the *Daily Mirror*, proved to be a great success in an expensive restaurant on rue Neuve, where our two tins of bully-beef were presented to the room at large on a giant silver salver, sliced as thin as a paper handkerchief, garnished with tomato and cucumber rings, and offered, at our request, to the elderly clientele who accepted with well-fed, but graceful, bows and nods.

The black market, it would appear, didn't run to bully-beef. Yet.

That was early September – ahead lay another city awaiting liberation.

This time we failed disastrously.

There was to be no liberation for Arnhem.

Another catastrophe.

I (seconded to an infantry division) sat in the mud and ice during a long, bitter winter just across the river while the Dutch starved to death on the other side.

This time the catastrophe was obvious. We had no need of the books the generals might later write to explain things. We saw it happen before our eyes, unwilling witnesses to a shattering disaster.

The euphoria of Paris and Brussels drained away. The tough times were back. It was just as well that I was aware of that fact for there was worse to come.

In April, as the last of the snows melted in the larch forests like strips of soiled bandage, we came to Belsen and the first concentration camp: a hideous 'liberation' this time which erased for ever the erroneous idea we had had that 'Jerry is really just the same as us'.

No way was he.

The war ended, for Christopher and me, not as I had somehow always thought it might, triumphantly in Berlin, but while we were sitting on a pile of logs in a pine forest near Lüneberg Heath, drinking coffee in tin mugs.

'Well, old dear,' said Chris. 'That's it. All done; all over.'

I had never felt so useless in my life.

In a letter to my father dated 7 May 1945, I wrote:

> ... It is the strangest feeling imaginable to know that it is over: one just idles about. There are no 'sorties' being flown so no work. And there won't be need of us, *or* our work, from now on. There is a weird vacuum: for so many months now it has been a fourteen or sixteen (sometimes twenty-four) hour day of strain and anxiety. All gone now. The in-built fear that someone somewhere might take a shot at you, or drop a bomb on you, has evaporated. There are still hazards about. Mines, and a band of zealots called Werewolves who are determined to fight on, but, apart from stringing piano wire across the roads thus decapitating one or two unfortunate blokes driving jeeps or motorcycles, they don't amount to much and most of them are kids anyway, about fifteen or so. So we don't worry much.
>
> Jodle apparently capitulated to Ike today in Rheims, and if that is so, that's that. I don't know quite what will happen to me now, it's been a bit sudden in some ways, but I expect I'll be given UK leave and then get shipped off to the Far East. There is still a war there. One sometimes forgets! It'll suit me in a way. I think I'll have a serious try at staying on with the Army: if I survive the next lot of course! I've enjoyed the companionship and the unexpected lack of res-

ponsibility. The Army, as far as it can, DOES take care of you, and I'm not at all certain now that I would ever be able to settle down among civilians again. I've got my books, a tent, a servant and a jeep. I honestly don't think I could be happier! But time will tell, it's very early days after all, and I *do* need a job to do. Maybe the planning for the fall of Singapore? It's in the air . . .

They swooped low, swung upwards in a spiralling loop, spun down, and scattered into glossy leaves of a banyan tree, screeching and squabbling as they settled to roost. Aunt Kitty's flights of scarlet birds across an opal sky.

These weren't scarlet – just ordinary green parrots – but the sky was opal, the high monsoon clouds were rising against the darkening sky, washed in carmine, orange, blue and green.

Over the verandah of the Mess, which had once been Tagore's house, peacocks planed down as gracefully and silently as hang-gliders to settle on the crumbling dome of a little temple buried in long grasses, marigolds and zinnias. They preened, bobbed, and fluttered their tails like foppish fans. Raindrops from the last heavy fall edged the leaves of the Canna lilies like diamonds.

Somewhere, from the very back of memory, these

sights were somehow familiar. Even to the monkeys who swung through the jacaranda trees baring yellow teeth in hideous grins, defecating in anger.

In the bazaar, across the compound, the sense of texture and scent which she had offered me all those years ago was mine in abundance: silks, cottons, linen, trembling voiles, blazing everywhere in colours far too brilliant for any northern light; and the scents of coriander, mace, clove and nutmeg, of flour and damp hemp, ghee, camel dung and patchouli, swamped the senses.

As the light failed, the wail of flutes and the tapping of drums mixed with the cries of the merchants and beggars, and the high laughter of children trailing kites.

A different world to the one I had left a few months ago, arriving as a Draft of One, to cross India and begin, as I had expected, to join the planning of Operation 'Zipper'.

Only there was no planning because the monsoon had arrived with me; and that meant no flights and no flights meant no sorties and so, workless, one idled through the humid days.

'Difficult to say what they'll do with you,' said Scotty rattling the ice-cubes in his gin-sling. 'No tell-ing really. Once we start off again, after the rains, we might get a clue – you'll probably be sent down to one of the Divisions, I shouldn't wonder. The bloody Japs have got their backs to the wall but they fight like hell.'

'So I have been told.'

'Sub-human, the buggers. For God's sake don't think otherwise. Monstrous people. Don't get taken prisoner. Take your cyanide pill instead.'

Remembering Belsen I said: 'The Germans weren't actually Fairy Twinkle Toes.'

'These are worse. Unfathomable. Savages. Bound four of our chaps with bailing wire into a tidy bundle, head to feet, doused them with petrol and set 'em alight. Alive.'

'Christ!'

'*He* wasn't around at the time; they've no pity, no mercy.' He drained his drink, tipped the melting ice-cubes into a potted palm. 'Should be exterminated like the vermin they are.' He got to his feet, pulled down the skirt of his bush-jacket.

'Want the other half of that?'

I followed him into the Mess.

Three nights later we heard that the bomb had been dropped on Hiroshima.

In the silence which greeted the news in the

crowded, still Mess, someone said: 'God Almighty! Now look what we've done, let the bloody genie out of the bottle, we'll never get it back in, never.'

Just for good measure they dropped another on Nagasaki three days after, and a week later the Japanese capitulated. The war was finally over.

If I had felt absolutely useless when Germany had surrendered, I felt worse now. There wasn't a war to fight and I wanted to stay on in the army: I was deeply thankful that I would not have to face the Japanese in battle - everything I had been told by the old hands had horrified me into incomprehension of so barbaric an enemy – but I consoled myself further by my awareness that there would be much to do in the areas which they had occupied and ravaged and in which they had spread their dreadful gospel of hate and vengeance.

Someday someone would send for me.

But they didn't: I was forgotten for the time being. The army had other things to do apart from worrying about one lone captain who wanted to stay on.

In the atmosphere of euphoria and exotic laziness, among the sights and sounds and scents, I drifted into an affair with a woman some years older than myself.

Nan was no starry-eyed girl. Quite the opposite: she knew very well, instinctively, that I was cautious, evasive, unwilling to be trapped. Afraid of possession.

So she played her cards supremely well, encouraging me to read, to write my dire poems, even (time was so heavy on our hands) to write a play, which she carefully typed out for me in the evenings in the now deserted office. She encouraged, flattered, suggested a brilliant future in civilian life, and almost convinced me that I should not remain with my regiment and stay in the army.

She never once, in all the plans which she laid for my future, included herself. Far too clever for that, she was certain that in a matter of time I would come to depend on her for so much that I should find it impossible to break the bond which she was carefully forging.

And the bond, at that time, was strong: we were inseparable, and she was fun. We danced at the Club almost every evening, spent all our time together, rode mules into Sikkim on a three-week trek which I planned could take us to Tibet because I had a great passion to see Lhasa. We never got to Tibet – that was forbidden territory – but at least we saw Everest and lay hand in hand under the stars and the deodars.

As far as our companions were concerned we were 'paired'. I think that Nan believed so too.

I did not. At nights, lying in the noisy darkness beneath my mosquito net, her body heavy in sleep beside me, the scent of 'Je Reviens' on her throat and shoulders, I felt a wrench of panic that I was entering a maze from which there could, decently, be no escape. My love for her was provisional only. I hadn't the remotest idea how to escape from an intense affair which I had helped create only to ease the tedium of my boredom and idleness, and which was now beginning to overwhelm me.

But the army had not forgotten me.

After three months, I was despatched to Java where, Scotty informed me with some degree of relish, they were 'having a hell of a time with a bloody civil war; the Japs surrendered to the Indonesians and *they* won't give the guns back to the Dutch! You'll have a very jolly time, old boy.'

Nan came down to Kidderpore Docks to see me off on the LST which was to carry me across the Equator.

'It seems very small to cross the Indian Ocean in,' she said. 'A walnut shell.'

'It is.'

'LST 3033. At least I know what you're in and where you are going.'

'Yes . . . keep your ears open; in case the fishes get me.'

'And you'll write? Remember, after the 27th of next month write to my sister's place. Ladbroke Grove. She'll keep them for me.'

'I will. As soon as I'm settled in.'

Somewhere among the jostling, feverish crowds on the quayside, someone shouted: 'Quit India! Quit India!'; others joined in waving clenched fists in the air at no one in particular.

'You'd better get away, they are starting to get restless. Bloody Congress, bloody Gandhi. Don't get stuck, go now.'

'I will. The gharri's there. Ladbroke Grove, remember?'

'After the 27th.'

I watched her walking straight-backed, but with a slight limp – the strap on her sandal had snapped. She carried it in one hand.

I knew that she wouldn't look back, and she did not. The bond had been broken.

I turned away as the engine started up, a dull throbbing shuddering up through the metal deck. I went below as a Draft of One: for Java.

•

We had crossed the equator in the early hours of the morning; I had set my tin alarm clock for 3.00 a.m. and went up on deck to watch. Some well-meaning idiot at the bar in Raffles Hotel the day before had assured me that there really was a visible line in the sea, and I had laughed, naturally; but none the less set an alarm clock.

To make sure.

And there was. Or so it pleased me to think.

Stars blazed from a jet sky and a half-moon appeared to cast a strange rippling line across the water: it was exactly as if two tides were meeting, riffling together, merging, shimmering in the heavy swell. It satisfied me, leaning over the thin iron rail of the ship.

I liked the idea, even though I knew perfectly well that it could only be an illusion. But then so much of my life in the last two or three years had seemed to be an illusion that one more wasn't going to upset my particular apple-cart. I accepted the line for a 'line', and that was that. I had, after all, *seen* a strange joining of the waters, like the interlocking of fingers, and that is how I would always remember it, and do.

Our snub-nosed LST cut through the phosphorescent waters with an elegant curl of white foam tumbling the wake behind us in folds of gold and silver.

Apart from the throb of engines far below my feet, and the soft creaking of a metal stanchion, there was no other sound except the swish and swirl of the sea against the hull.

I felt strangely alone, exceedingly rich, drenched in these sights and gentle sounds with no one in the world to share them, and no one to shatter the beauty by comment and the banality of human speech. That kind of beauty needs no underlining.

It just is. Perfect, complete, rare, unshareable.

Far away to starboard a tiny light flashed with the regularity of a metronome. A lighthouse on the coast of Sumatra, brighter even than the stars.

We slid across the 'visible' line through the glittering night, with the Southern Cross tilted high above, into equatorial waters.

I had come a long way from Great Meadow and the Cottage, from the mud-scented delights of the river at Twickenham, from the grey conformity of the Anthracite Years which had been, after all, the anvil on which my strength, such as it was, had been forged.

I knew that tomorrow all this glory would be memory, which is probably why I spent so much time on that deck memorizing it for ever, imprinting it on my mind so that wherever I went, whatever became of me, as long as I should be breathing and aware, I could remember and in remembering be enriched once again.

My short stay in Singapore during the last two days had heightened my sense of awareness, re-reminding me that life is at best ephemeral, at worst too easily lost and rubbished into oblivion: tomorrow, I knew, I should land on a strange island, wrenched by strife, anguish, bitterness and blind hatred, to take my part as a 'policeman', nothing else, in the bloody shaping of its future.

It seemed to me at the time a pretty daunting enterprise, and unworkable, which so it proved to be eventually, but I had no sense of fear then, or the remotest apprehension: it was a job which I should enjoy somehow, even though I would be forbidden to fire a shot in anger, even to protect myself.

I knew, of course, that it was almost impossible, indeed it *was* impossible, to try and impose law and order on a country hell-bent in ridding itself of colonial rule. I'd seen a good deal of that already in India with the rioting of the Congress Party. If the wretched island to which I was presently on my way wanted its Dutch rulers out, there was nothing, I knew, that anyone, however well-meaning and however imbued with a sense of order and control, could do to stop the surging masses, hysterical with slogans and blood-lust.

In Calcutta one afternoon I had seen the kind of fury that lay just beneath the surface of apparent orderliness when a Hindu youth of about sixteen jumped a food queue and was, there and then, hacked limb from limb in the busy street. There was no quarter, no mercy, no possibility of law or order, no reasoning.

Nan had grabbed my cap and buried her face, trying at the same time to cover her ears so that the screams could, at least, be muffled.

No one tried to help; but then, no one ever did.

We stood trapped in the seething, screaming crowd.

The youth's trunk lay bloodily in the gutter, head savagely battered, hair matted, eyes staring wide in surprise among an incongruous litter of old confetti and orange peel.

It was a fairly common occurrence in those days; mob violence was only a skin's-depth away, and incidents such as this were just the lid rattling on the boiling pot.

Caught in such a situation, the wisest thing to do was to try to ease oneself away as discreetly and quietly as possible; *never* push or hurry; walk slowly.

Capless, I led a weeping Nan through the shouting crowd; her long hair had fallen about her face and shoulders in an untidy cascade, and this probably helped our departure, for we were unrecognizable as officers of His Majesty's detested services by the jostling, screaming horde with its foam-frilled lips.

In India we knew that the fuse was short, the mechanism ticking, the bomb gigantic. When we left, as leave we knew we must, a tidal wave of hatred, violence and heedless frenzy would sweep the great continent, and Hindu and Muslim would only stop to catch their breaths when the killings were done.

The Indian Christians, and the terrified Eurasians, knew this equally well, and begged constantly for help, to be allowed to leave with us when we went, but no one gave a fig for them frankly; no one even bothered to do anything about them.

When we left we'd lower all the flags and quit, and then, as someone said in the Mess one night: 'We'll let the inmates run the bloody asylum, sort it out among themselves – they won't be able to, of course, but let the buggers try if that's what they want.'

It was a sentiment frequently expressed by a great number of men in the army who had come out from Britain to hold India against a Japanese invasion.

It was a negative approach of course – but then India induces negativity.

Standing on the deck that night, now so long ago, I remember being very glad that I had left the country at last; I knew that the official war was over, that the Japanese had surrendered, and that I had chucked my cyanide pill into the sea long since. *That* fact comforted me very much indeed.

I was sailing to a new job as a 'policeman', and if that was the role I had to play, so be it – it was a great deal better than having to fight the Japs, for I knew that if that had been my fate I could never have survived.

I felt pretty certain (wrongly of course) that it would be a fairly peaceful affair; I'd be there to assist in collecting the lost POWs and the Dutch internees (that had been my briefing in Calcutta) and help get them safely home. Nothing to it really – almost a Red Cross job.

So there I stood against the rail, filled with contentment by the splendour of the night all about me, and a feeling that the worst was over, and that I had survived: so far.

I waited until the first thin thread of scarlet day split the night on the portside horizon, beyond Borneo.

I was linked with my earliest memories; for these were Aunt Kitty's islands and already, in my imagination, they were half familiar.

I thought.

It is true that defeat has an odour.

It meandered through the paint-peeling streets of Singapore like a slowly dispersing marsh gas, lying in pockets here and there, loitering in rooms and corridors, bitter, clinging, sickening.

We docked in Keppel harbour: rusted cranes, a half-sunken steamer, ruined warehouses with hollow, bullet-pocked façades. Military trucks, piles of stores, oil drums, a Union Jack hanging limply from a pole. It was five weeks after the Japanese surrender.

Beyond the wrecked buildings, which lined the dockyard like a row of rotten teeth, the towers, palms and pinnacles of the city struck hard against the intensity of the blue sky; sampans criss-crossed the oily waters like waterboatmen, and birds, strange to me, mewed and cried, swooping low above the churning wake of our LST.

The day was already hot and humid when I set off through the dockyard to go and see the city which had 'died' so ignominiously in the February of 1942.

A whitewashed bastard Tunbridge Wells – with palm trees.

Domed, arched, turreted, pillared, apparently empty.

Miss Havisham's wedding cake crumbling in defeat and cobwebs after three and a half years of Japanese occupation.

On the Singapore River Chinese life, however, went its way in a tidy explosion of activity.

Sampans jammed the muddy waters like the tumble of a thousand dominoes spilled along the winding fringes of the riverbanks.

In Chinatown proper, washing hung from every window and balcony, or from bamboo poles thrust out across the narrow streets; shutters were bleached by years of sun and tropical rains, some had never been opened, others hung like lolling tongues. On the shops, Chinese lettering danced and sprang in scarlet strokes in the brilliant light, and rickshaws and bicycles bounced over the pot-holes in the twisting alleys, tinny bells furiously ringing, weaving through crowds of laughing, playing children, as innocent as butterfly swarms.

Among this cheerful chaos, ramshackle stalls were piled with all kinds of goods, from dried mushrooms and rice to Japanese whisky and scrawny hens bunched alive, hanging by their legs looking anxious. Everywhere there was the cloying smell of frying oil and dried fish, heavy on the morning air, but above all there was activity and life.

The European quarter was different.

A deserted Sunday afternoon lethargy. Some military personnel here and there, jeeps and trucks revving up, turning, tail-boards clattering noisily in the almost deserted streets, Robinsons Department Store (the Harrods of the East, they said) had been struck by bombs and stared in sullen shock across the silent street with empty eyes: sockets in a scabbed, decaying face.

The city smelled of drains, damp and desolation. The mustiness of a long-closed room. My booted footsteps cracked back in echo in the stillness.

In Raffles Place there was a small parked Austin car with rusted chrome and a flat tyre, and two Chinese men in flip-flops carrying a bamboo ladder.

Far above, in the dazzle of the morning sky, kites planed and swung, coasting in the currents of higher air.

Beyond the cricket club grounds, rutted and worn,
 St Andrew's Cathedral crouched in abandoned grace

surrounded by a filigree of jacaranda and flame trees, as alien and out of place as a swan on the Ganges, and all around the pompous pillared buildings, heavy with swagged stone urns and porticos, stood silent, vacant, blind – their Colonial grandeur humbled as if they too, like the occupants who had been forced to leave them, had also 'lost face'.

I hitched a lift on a truck to Tanglin Barracks and the Club; we drove through wincingly genteel suburbs, past gable-beamed and pebbledashed houses with names like 'Fairholm' and 'The Paddocks', buried now in bougainvillaea and flame trees, the jungle already weaving lianas through shattered verandahs, and thrusting bamboo thickets across long-forgotten lawns and rose gardens.

Some had been used as desperate, hopeless strong-points in a lost battle. Blackened shells, incongruous chimney stacks striking up through charred beams, latticed windows swinging urgently in the stiff breeze which rustled the sword-like spikes of the palms. Some stood in an almost pristine state of suburban elegance, and these, my companions told me, had been used as Happy Homes for the Japanese rank and file; but the sounds of feminine laughter and the whisper of silken kimonos had dispersed into the air as surely as the 'thwack!' and 'thwock!' of tennis balls on the overgrown courts of the 'unconquerable' memsahibs.

In the almost empty bar of the Tanglin Club a friendly Australian ex-POW came over and offered to 'buy you a round, okeydoke?'

Ronnie had a long face and no teeth. 'Rifle butt; I answered back.' His skin was drum-taut over angular bones, his joints, elbows and knees were swollen like melons on arms and legs as thick as drinking-straws, his new jungle green uniform hung on his tall, bony frame like a tent.

'Been here since '42. We arrived just as the bloody place folded up. Great bit of timing. Shoved us up into the rubber and said: "Dig defences", but there weren't any shovels and the English bastard who owned the plantation said we'd be fined if we so much as laid a finger on one of his fuckin' trees. I ask you! The bloody Japs were up the road. Fined! Christ! This was the island that *no one* could touch. It was impregnable. Took me a day to work out what that word meant and by the time I had it didn't bloody matter anymore, it didn't apply. The Empire the sun never sets on they all said. Trouble was they didn't know a fuckin' sunset when they saw one.'

 'I thought you had all been repatriated?'

'Yah, we've nearly all gone. I go Wednesday and I tell you one thing, cobber, I won't be coming back, never want to see this sodding country ever again. I just survived, by the grace of God, and next time they can stuff their bleeding Empire.'

'I think they have.'

'I think so too. Good on 'em. When did you land?'

I told him and signalled for the unsmiling Malayan boy in his white jacket and ordered another round.

'Timed it really nice. All over bar the shouting, right? You know there's one thing saved our bacon: those bombs. If you lot had tried an invasion, know what the Japs were going to do? Kill all their prisoners – men, women, kids . . . mind you, they'd been doing their best to do it for nearly four years, but that's what we heard. Wipe us all out. The day they dropped that bomb was the best day that I can remember.'

He spoke quietly, in a tired level voice; there was no anger left in him. 'Only thing is,' he said, pushing his empty glass round in circles on the table, 'only thing I say is, they should have dropped twenty more, wiped the bastards off the face of the earth, because you know why? One day they'll try it again; betcha. All jammed on to those fuckin' little islands. Breeding like rats, they'll be falling off the edges soon, and then what? Plenty of room in Australia, it's dead *empty*. Get me?'

I got him. I was unshocked. The quietness of his voice and the authority with which he spoke of terrible things defused argument.

'Well, not for a while,' I said.

The boy came back with two bottles of Tiger beer and set them on the table. Ronnie began to refill his glass, his hands shook slightly.

'Maybe. Not for a while,' he said. 'If I'm talkin' funny it's because of no teeth, sorry, mate. You stuck here long? Singapore?'

'Leave for Java, day after tomorrow.'

'Good on you. No place to stay: they're all so bloody ashamed here. Lost face you see, and the Malays and Chinks *know* it. Doesn't do to "lose face", it isn't forgotten. Never in front of the natives.'

He sipped his beer for a moment in silence. Put his glass down. 'The men are all right, not too bad, the civvies, I mean. It's the bloody women, they are the worst, they ran this place. They didn't come here with smiling faces, they came here as bloody rulers. Do this! Get that! Rule Britannia! Christ!'

A small boy with a rubber inner-tube round his middle clambered out of the swimming-pool beside us and came across to the table, his wet hair dripping. He wiped his nose on the back of his hand, pointed to a small dish of rice-cookies.

'Can I have those?'

I pushed the dish towards him and he took a handful, without thanks.

A pale, blonde woman, at the far end of the pool, lying on a Lilo, suddenly sat up in her bathing costume, one arm across her breasts. She wasn't bad, long hair, a drawn face, thin, looking angry and embarrassed all at the same time.

'Jeremy!' she called. 'Jeremy! Come here, I told you not to. They're *soldiers*, come back at once.' A voice as harsh as a cane striking steel: meant for us to hear.

The boy swivelled slowly on his heels and went back to her pushing cookies into his mouth. She said something to him, slapped the cookies out of his hand, lay back.

Ronnie shrugged, sipped his beer. 'See what I mean? Really got a complex, all of them.'

Not all of them however: Mrs McCrombie hadn't any complexes whatsoever, at least as far as I could see. If she had, then she hid them quite admirably.

She was sitting on the lawns of Raffles Hotel in a

Lloyd Loom chair, wearing a man's khaki shirt and khaki slacks, a red ribbon tied about her short, iron-grey hair, face as wrinkled as a winter apple, eyes as sharp and blue as sapphires, and she smiled a lot.

She was, I suppose, then, about sixty-five or so (old in my youthful opinion). Her husband, David, who had survived the ordeal of Changi Jail, had gone up-country to see what, if anything, remained of the rubber plantations of which he was once the manager, and she had settled for a readjustment to life with friends in a small flat in the city after four years in Syme Road Camp.

'Frankly,' she said, 'I hope he *doesn't* find anything worth saving up there. He's most terribly conscientious of course, but I really have a *terrific* hankering for home – home's in Dorset. Near Corfe, do y'know it?'

'Very well. My father used to paint there a lot.'

'Artist, was he? Oh, we had masses of them. I expect you knew the Greyhound pub then?'

'Lord, yes! Smiths crisps and ice cream soda; shandy when I got bigger.'

'The crisps,' she said, 'with those little twists of salt in blue paper.'

For a moment I realized that I had lost her, she had drifted away, her eyes looking beyond the staff cars and manoeuvring trucks on the carriage drive of the hotel.

Unseeing; a tiny smile trembling.

Suddenly she rubbed her forehead nervously, almost with irritation, adjusted the red ribbon, smiled back at me.

'Sorry. I went off somewhere. It was all such a dreadful muddle here, you know. People *do* behave in the oddest ways in times of trouble. I mean to say, here in this place, they were dancing and playing tennis just as if nothing was happening! The Japs had crossed the Causeway, and we'd pulled out of the naval base leaving it quite undamaged! David saw it. Everything intact. It was madness.'

'Did they really come across on bicycles, the Japs?'

'Oh yes! That's quite, quite true. Hundreds of the blighters spinning along on those dreadful little Japanese bikes. Can you imagine? *We* couldn't. No one here did – we never thought of that, naturally. Bikes! They are, of course, the *most* ingenious people – quite caught us on the hop.' She laughed suddenly, like a dry cough. 'Hop!' she said. 'That's what they did, and that's what we were doing, or they were doing. Dancing. Tennis.

Funny. Do you know a dance tune, something called, was it "Deep Purple"?'

'Oh yes. Yes I know that.'

'I hate it,' she said.

A stiff breeze from the sea wrestled with the traveller's trees stuck along the edges of the lawn, snapped the Union Jack on its pole above the façade.

She looked up at it.

'Nice to see it back again.' She folded her arms on the table top. 'We had to kill the dogs. I think that was almost the worst thing really.'

'The dogs?'

'Well, when we realized that it was the end, David and I knew what we had to do; he got the Humber out and we took the dogs to the vet.' She leant forward, her hands cupping her face.

'They thought they were going for "walkies". You know? They adored the car an' all. But of course everyone else had the same idea at the same time. There was a queue of cars simply miles long; people walking too; weeping. So many dogs. All kinds. Tongues hanging out, pulling at their leashes, some being dragged. They were anxious, aware of our grief. Dogs are; did you know? They sense one's anxiety, one's fear, one's

distress. Of course you got the odd Jack Russell behaving badly, snarling and jumping at everyone. Terror I imagine – most of them knew what was happening. I know that mine did. Barney was trembling from head to foot, and Rollo, he was David's dog, just stayed close to him, his head jammed tight against his master. He never moved from him. Never.'

She cleared her throat, placed her arms on the table top again. 'Poor people. The vets were dead with exhaustion. Collies, spaniels, Airedales, pekes, all kinds . . . so many – but we simply had to do it; had to.' She sat back in the Lloyd Loom chair and when she spoke again her voice was firm and brisk.

'*You* don't want to hear all these awful things! Too depressing – all in the past now anyway. Gosh!' she said, her eyes sparkling. 'We *were* glad that you all got here when you did! I don't think that we could have managed for very much longer really, things were getting pretty grim. We *were* glad! Oh goodness yes!'

'I'm afraid I wasn't here for the Liberation. I'm on my way down to Java, I only got in yesterday.'

'Well. You know what I mean, don't you? All of you, so young and fresh, so strong; we really never thought it possible towards the very end. There *was* a rumour that they would kill us all. Too many mouths to feed and what to do with us if you had invaded, you know? And then that bomb was dropped; after that it was different. But before, in the dreadful days, goodness what muddles! No one knew what to do, and when the *Repulse* and the poor *Prince of Wales* went down, that was pretty well that. No navy, no air force to speak of, and the Japs were so *much* stronger than we were, thousands of them swarming all over the place. We hadn't a chance. Just caved in, I'm afraid.'

She laughed shortly. Pushed the ribbon about on her forehead. 'Not *really* the sort of thing to tell one's grandchildren, is it?'

Long, long after the disaster of the Falaise Gap in Normandy, we learned just what had happened there; and long after my meeting with Mrs McCrombie, and long after I had stood miserably in the fog on Guildford station, I discovered what had actually happened in Singapore, and why the British were so deeply shamed and, as Ronnie had told me, 'lost face'.

Lieutenant General Yamashita, commanding the Japanese forces at that time, was outnumbered by three to one, short of supplies and exhausted. If he had had to hold on and face a counter-attack, he admitted later, he would have lost, and the greatest military disaster in history, as it has since been called, would never have occurred.

But no one knew at the time. And there was no thought of a counter-attack.

Hindsight is a woeful word.

So, as in Normandy, as in Malaya. Those in the middle of things didn't know. Bickering, squabbling, incompetence, absurd snobbery and idiotic arrogance caused the deaths of thousands of men and lost the British their Empire – perhaps not immediately, but the chocks had been kicked away and the ship of state, so to speak, was on the move down the slipway to disaster.

I have always thought that it would have been comforting to think that Mrs McCrombie, and others like her, would never learn the true facts; but if she survived I suppose that, inevitably, she did.

But thousands upon thousands would never know – would never realize that it had all been in vain finally. There are no learned revelations for the dead.

Near the District Commissioner's tennis court in Kohima there is a modest memorial to all those who died in that campaign. It carries a simple message, four lines long:

When you go home
Tell them of us and say
For your tomorrow
We gave our today.

Who goes now to Kohima?

After I had done my stint as a 'policeman' in Java, I returned once again to Singapore and Tanglin Barracks, waiting for a berth back to England and repatriation.

Many changes had taken place since my first visit. The streets were busy again; Orchard Road was jammed with trucks, cars and rickshaws; ENSA was installed; there were scores of tatty little restaurants 'In Bounds to HM Forces'; people were dancing again at The Happy World; Raffles Hotel stated, on a discreet card, that 'If you are wearing HM Uniform you are not welcome'; and there was a subtle, understated, segregation of Singapore civilians and military personnel in the Tanglin Club, part of which had been commandeered as an Officers' Club, where the dough-kneed newcomers (with one Defence Medal up) sat about in their over-starched shorts drinking Tiger beer and gin-slings, talking too loudly; and in the city, Kelly and Walshe's splendid bookshop had opened up again with new deliveries of books from America and Britain.

It was there that I went to find something to read on the long seven-week voyage home. I found just what I needed: a copy of *Gone With the Wind*. As I put out my hand to take it, a neatly gloved woman's hand reached towards it at the same moment.

I instantly withdrew mine, and offered her the book politely.

She was a middle-aged woman, straight-backed, grey-haired, in a blue tussore suit and a blue straw hat, a handbag in the crook of her elbow.

I can see her in this room now – at this very moment.

She turned abruptly away from me, and calling down the entire length of the shop, to a startled assistant, she said: 'Boy! Tell this officer that if he wishes to address me, to do so through you.'

Not everything had changed in Singapore.

Major-General Douglas Hawthorn, DSO, was not standing with open arms to greet me as we docked at Tandjoeng Priok. To be perfectly fair he had no idea that I was coming to join his Division.

No one else had either, for that matter.

The place was swarming with people of all kinds and colours, with tanks and trucks, with perspiring coolies, with running Japanese in little squads, naked save for their boots, peaked caps and flapping loin-cloths, with jeeps jolting over the rubbled concrete, with turbaned Indians and tall, bony British military police in crisp green uniforms and gleaming white lanyards. A bewildering crowd scene overwhelmed by the acrid stink of burning rubber and the more subtle, and far harder to identify individually, scent of spices.

With my tin trunk, portable typewriter and a canvas suitcase I stood abandoned in the midst of carnival. Unwanted, unplaced, unexpected.

A military policeman, with a ginger moustache and the disdain of a llama, led me to the office where, he said, with no degree of certainty: 'Someone will sort it out for you.'

The office was sweltering, even at this early hour, and a pallid corporal, with skin as translucent and as pale as a potato shoot, wearily looked up from some files.

'Any idea where they are? Your people?'

'None. I was sent down from Calcutta; told to report to 23 Indian Div. HQ.'

'Could be anywhere. I'm new myself. Calcutta, did you say?'

'Yes.'

'Long way, sir.'

'Long enough.'

'You come in on 3033, did you?'

'I did. She's unloading over there.'

'Dicey trip.'

'Oh. Why dicey?'

'Submarines, sir.' He was rustling papers. 'They say that there are Jap subs all over the place and that some of them don't know, or won't believe, there's been a surrender. Could have been nasty, if you see what I mean.'

'Very. I can't swim.'

He looked up sharply, a paper in his hand. 'Not much point in swimming. That sea is stiff with sharks.' He went to his telephone. 'Got some "gen" here, we won't be long now.'

Two hours later I was still sitting on my tin trunk, wreathed in the fumes of rubber smoke and spices; but any thoughts of Aunt Kitty's magical islands in the Indian Ocean had long been dispersed.

The subaltern who finally arrived helped me load my gear, and started off through the swarming crowds. He was disinclined to talk, but offered the excuse that he had been on night duty, was bushed, and that no one knew I was coming.

As if I hadn't realized this with blinding clarity some hours before.

The sky grew darker as we got nearer the City, the sun floated, an aluminium disc, behind the heavy pall of smoke which hung above the distant buildings like a wavering canopy.

The traffic was intense, the subaltern's driving alarming, the roads pot-holed, swarming with dogs and children, rickshaws and bicycles, sagging electric light cables and heavy trucks pushing through heedlessly; he suggested that I hold on tight.

'Extremists,' he said suddenly, indicating the billowing cloud of smoke under which we now were weaving an intricate, and near-suicidal, path. 'They hit a rubberstore last night, got the oil depot the night before, hacked thirty internees to bits near Bekassi, and you'd better watch out for landmines – *and* grenades. They chuck them about like ping-pong balls, all in the name of freedom. It's not like Margate.'

I wondered why on earth he would have thought I might think it was. But said nothing. I was dispirited enough without this generous information.

A small villa in a suburban street, standing in a long-abandoned quarter-acre was where I finally landed. This was 'A' Mess. It said so on a piece of cardboard nailed to a pole in the front garden.

In a prim, almost empty little room, with sun-rotted lace curtains at the bay window, a picture of a windmill and a canal on one wall, and a rusty tin garden table against another, a silent, but grinning, Gurkha with an embarrassment of gold teeth unpacked my kit, erected my camp bed and mosquito net, and indicated that his name was Goa.

As far as I could comprehend, for we had no common tongue, and it was only by his pointing to himself with his finger and repeating an incomprehensible string of words that I was able to isolate, phonetically, an assumed name, Goa.

Goa he remained for the rest of my tour of duty, and I came to love him dearly. When the time arrived, eventually, for me to leave Java, Goa smuggled himself, and his kit, into my transport to the docks and pleaded to be allowed to come with me to England. He was splendidly smart, his brasses gleamed, his belt was blanco'd, his boots shone, his tears streamed down his cheeks.

By this time, a year later, we had invented a strange form of language which we used together. Anyone listening to us would not have understood a word, but we did. Which is, after all, what mattered.

'No, Goa. No – *Sahib go*. Not possible Goa go.'

For a moment he looked at me in stubborn silence.

'Goa stay along Pip-sahib. Stay along.'

'Pip-sahib go along Britain. *Tikh hai?*'

He suddenly fumbled in the pocket of his battledress jacket and brought out a worn and tattered piece of card. Stuck on it was a photograph of King George and Queen Elizabeth cut from a magazine.

He held it out to me, then turned it towards himself at arm's length, drew himself to attention, and saluted.

'Goa, go. Look-see burra sahib. Burra, burra sahib Brit-inn. Okay?'

'*Not*-okay. Not good. Goa not go. Goa rest along Division. Is *duty. Tikh hai?*'

He looked at me with such bewildered pain and distress that I felt a lump rise in my throat as large as a fist.

Our 'language' was far too limited to explain why he could not come with me to see his King.

He stood perfectly still, then replaced the piece of card, never once taking his eyes from mine, rebuttoned his pocket, moved one pace back, slammed to attention in his brilliantly polished boots, saluted, turned on his heel, hoisted his kitbag over one shoulder, and was lost in the jostling crowd pushing about at the foot of the gang-plank.

He'd gone. And I never saw him again.

 He had been 'allotted' to me temporarily, at first,

because he was considered to be hot-tempered, difficult, stubborn – and he was all these things, but we grew fond of each other and respected each other. In some strange way we made a pattern of life together which worked well: he retained his pride at all times while serving as my batman-driver, which must have been difficult for him because he was a fierce, brave fighting man, and it was never his wish to be a servant.

No one else was anxious to have him for the simple reason that he had removed the head of his last officer, neatly, with a single swipe of his *kukri* while the man was asleep. Apparently there was good reason for this extravagant act, for the officer had, in some way which was never fully explained to me, insulted Goa, his bravery, his religion and his race. The whole ugly affair had been hushed up and dealt with discreetly within the Division, for it was well known that Goa was a fair and fearless man, and had shown incredible bravery and courage in battle from Imphal onwards.

The story may, indeed, have been apocryphal, but I accepted it as true. It was far more interesting.

He was proud, funny, devoted to the Division, kind and at all times passionately loyal to his King. He was, I imagine, in his early forties and had a wife and three sons in the hills of Nepal and I can only hope that he got back to them safely in the end.

And forgave me for leaving him behind.

There is a profound difference between being 'alone' and 'lonely'.

I was both for the first few days after my arrival in the Division, stuck in one or other of the three bleak little villas which constituted 'A' Mess. My brother officers were perfectly civil at all times, but there was a clear feeling that I was an outsider among a group of people who had fought together, and suffered heavy casualties doing so, in bitter and costly battles up on the Assam–Burma border, which they had secured against the Japanese.

I knew nothing of their war, they knew nothing of mine in Europe. I spoke English only, no Urdu or Malayan. We had absolutely nothing in common. The problems which they found in Java were not what they had expected at all. It was by no means (as *I* had cheerfully thought on my LST) simply a matter of being a 'policeman' and shunting POWs and Dutch internees back to Singapore and doing, as I had been told earlier, a simple Red Cross job.

It was far graver than that.

PENGUIN 60s

PENGUIN 60s

LAURIE LEE · *To War in Spain*
PATRICK LEIGH FERMOR · *Loose as the Wind*
ELMORE LEONARD · *Trouble at Rindo's Station*
DAVID LODGE · *Surprised by Summer*
BERNARD MAC LAVERTY · *The Miraculous Candidate*
SHENA MACKAY · *Cloud-Cuckoo-Land*
NORMAN MAILER · *The Dressing Room*
PETER MAYLE · *Postcards from Summer*
JAN MORRIS · *Scenes from Havian Life*
BLAKE MORRISON · *Camp Cuba*
VLADIMIR NABOKOV · *Now Remember*
REDMOND O'HANLON · *A River in Borneo*
STEVEN PINKER · *Thinking in Tongues*
CRAIG RAINE · *Private View*
CLAUDIA RODEN · *Ful Medames and Other Vegetarian Dishes*
HELGE RUBINSTEIN · *Chocolate Parfait*
SIMON SCHAMA · *The Taking of the Bastille*
WILL SELF · *The Rock of Crack As Big As the Ritz*
MARK SHAND · *Elephant Tales*
NIGEL SLATER · *30-Minute Suppers*
RICK STEIN · *Fresh from the Sea*
LYTTON STRACHEY · *Florence Nightingale*
PAUL THEROUX · *Slow Trains to Simla*
COLIN THUBRON · *Samarkand*
MARK TULLY · *Beyond Purdah*
LAURENS VAN DER POST · *Merry Christmas, Mr Lawrence*
MARGARET VISSER · *More than Meets the Eye*
GAVIN YOUNG · *Something of Samoa*

and

Thirty Obituaries from Wisden · SELECTED BY MATTHEW ENGEL

READ MORE IN PENGUIN

For complete information about books available from Penguin and how to order them, please write to us at the appropriate address below. Please note that for copyright reasons the selection of books varies from country to country.

IN THE UNITED KINGDOM: Please write to *Dept. EP, Penguin Books Ltd, Bath Road, Harmondsworth, Middlesex UB7 ODA.*

IN THE UNITED STATES: Please write to *Consumer Sales, Penguin USA, P.O. Box 999, Dept. 17109, Bergenfield, New Jersey 07621-0120.* VISA and MasterCard holders call 1-800-253-6476 to order Penguin titles.

IN CANADA: Please write to *Penguin Books Canada Ltd, 10 Alcorn Avenue, Suite 300, Toronto, Ontario M4V 3B2.*

IN AUSTRALIA: Please write to *Penguin Books Australia Ltd, P.O. Box 257, Ringwood, Victoria 3134.*

IN NEW ZEALAND: Please write to *Penguin Books (NZ) Ltd, Private Bag 102902, North Shore Mail Centre, Auckland 10.*

IN INDIA: Please write to *Penguin Books India Pvt Ltd, 706 Eros Apartments, 56 Nehru Place, New Delhi 110 019.*

IN THE NETHERLANDS: Please write to *Penguin Books Netherlands bv, Postbus 3507, NL-1001 AH Amsterdam.*

IN GERMANY: Please write to *Penguin Books Deutschland GmbH, Metzlerstrasse 26, 60594 Frankfurt am Main.*

IN SPAIN: Please write to *Penguin Books S. A., Bravo Murillo 19, 1° B, 28015 Madrid.*

IN ITALY: Please write to *Penguin Italia s.r.l., Via Felice Casati 20, I-20124 Milano.*

IN FRANCE: Please write to *Penguin France S. A., 17 rue Lejeune, F-31000 Toulouse.*

IN JAPAN: Please write to *Penguin Books Japan, Ishikiribashi Building, 2-5-4, Suido, Bunkyo-ku, Tokyo 112.*

IN GREECE: Please write to *Penguin Hellas Ltd, Dimocritou 3, GR-106 71 Athens.*

IN SOUTH AFRICA: Please write to *Longman Penguin Southern Africa (Pty) Ltd, Private Bag X08, Bertsham 2013.*